How Social Media Shapes Our Lives and Relationships?

C. P. Kumar
Reiki Healer
Roorkee - 247667, India

Disclaimer

While every effort has been made to ensure the accuracy and completeness of the content in this book, the author cannot guarantee that the information contained herein is error-free, up-to-date, or suitable for every individual circumstance.

The author shall not be held liable or responsible for any errors or omissions in the content of the book, nor for any damages, or losses that may arise from any actions taken based upon the suggestions or contents presented in the book.

Readers are advised to use their own judgment and discretion in applying the information provided in this book, and to consult with qualified professionals before taking any action based on the contents of this book. The author disclaims any and all liability or responsibility for any actions taken or not taken based on the information contained in this book.

DEDICATION

To those who navigate the digital landscapes of connection and community, this book is dedicated to you - the explorers, the storytellers, and the architects of our virtual societies. In the ever-evolving realm of social media, where each click and share contributes to the mosaic of our shared experiences, your presence and participation shape the fabric of our interconnected lives.

May this exploration into the chapters of "How Social Media Shapes Our Lives and Relationships" serve as a guide through the landscape of pixels and emotions. To the pioneers who have witnessed the birth and growth of social media, to the trailblazers charting its unexplored territories, and to those who seek to understand the profound impact on our identities, relationships, and societies - this book is a tribute to your curiosity and resilience.

In the spirit of connection that social media fosters, this dedication extends to the diverse voices that weave the rich tapestry of our global conversations. As we delve into the complexities of online interactions, may we reflect on the responsibility we bear in shaping the digital world and, in turn, acknowledge the power it holds over our lives.

To all those who strive to maintain balance in the age of constant connectivity, who confront challenges with resilience, and who contribute to fostering positive change within these virtual spaces, your presence in this digital narrative is invaluable. This book stands as a testament to the importance of understanding, navigating, and harnessing the influence of social media on our lives and relationships.

In gratitude for the shared journey through the landscapes of the internet and the boundless potential it holds for connection, communication, and collaboration. May our digital endeavors continue to reflect the best of humanity as we shape the future of social media together.

With heartfelt appreciation,

C. P. Kumar

CONTENTS

PREFACE

In the vast landscape of the digital age, where connectivity transcends geographical boundaries and communication is just a click away, social media has emerged as a powerful force shaping the very fabric of our lives and relationships. This book, "How Social Media Shapes Our Lives and Relationships", delves into the intricate interplay between our digital existence and the dynamics of our personal connections.

The journey begins with an exploration of the roots of social media, tracing its humble beginnings to the sprawling network of platforms that dominate our online experiences today. Through a historical lens, we unravel the evolution of these platforms, each iteration a reflection of the changing tides of technology and society.

As we navigate the chapters ahead, the rise of social media takes center stage. We examine the staggering popularity and growth of these platforms, delving into the statistics and demographics that illuminate the vast and diverse user base. It becomes evident that social media is not merely a technological phenomenon but a cultural and societal force that resonates with individuals across the globe.

One of the most profound impacts of social media is its influence on our identity. In the digital realm, we shape and are shaped by our online personas. The book delves into the complex relationship between social media and self-identity, exploring how personal branding has become an integral part of the online experience.

Moving beyond the individual, the narrative unfolds to reveal the profound influence of social media on our relationships. From friendships and family connections to the intricate dance of love and romance, we scrutinize the ways in which social media both enriches and challenges the bonds that define us.

Yet, this digital landscape is not without its shadows. The book confronts the darker side of social media, examining the relationship between its use and mental health. We tackle the daunting challenges of cyberbullying and online harassment, offering insights on coping mechanisms and strategies for combating the digital perils that lurk in the shadows.

In the realm of politics, social media has become a formidable player, shaping opinions and influencing outcomes. We unravel the intricate threads connecting social media and the political landscape, exploring the consequences of misinformation and the challenges it poses to our democratic societies.

As we traverse the virtual landscape, concerns about privacy arise. The book scrutinizes the delicate balance between our online presence and the safeguarding of our personal data, providing practical tips on how to navigate the digital world without compromising our privacy.

The journey continues into the depths of addiction and dependency, examining the addictive nature of social media and offering practical advice for managing our online presence in a healthy way.

In a world where parenting faces unprecedented challenges, we explore the complexities of raising children in the social media age. From screen time struggles to the delicate balance between virtual and real-world experiences, we navigate the uncharted waters of modern parenthood.

The narrative culminates in an exploration of the economic impact of social media and its profound influence on consumer behavior. Finally, we gaze into the crystal ball, speculating on emerging trends and technologies that will shape the future of social media.

This book is a comprehensive guide, a navigation tool through the ever-evolving landscape of social media. It is an invitation to reflect, learn, and engage in the dialogue surrounding the profound ways in which social media has become an integral part of our lives and relationships. Welcome to a journey into the heart of the digital age.

C. P. Kumar
Reiki Healer
Former Scientist 'G', National Institute of Hydrology
Roorkee - 247667, India
Web: https://www.angelfire.com/nh/cpkumar/virgo.html

Chapter 1. Introduction to Social Media

In the vast landscape of the digital age, social media has emerged as a transformative force, redefining the way we communicate, connect, and perceive the world around us. As we delve into the intricate web of virtual interactions, it becomes imperative to understand the origins, evolution, and the profound impact that social media wields on our lives and relationships.

A Brief History of Social Media

The roots of social media can be traced back to the early days of the internet when platforms like SixDegrees, launched in 1997, laid the groundwork for virtual social connections. However, it was not until the advent of Friendster in 2003 that the term "social networking" gained mainstream recognition. Friendster's success paved the way for the juggernaut that followed — MySpace. This platform, known for its customizable profiles and music integration, captivated a global audience.

The real game-changer, however, emerged in 2004 with the inception of Facebook by Mark Zuckerberg and his college roommates. Facebook's meteoric rise marked the beginning of an era where social media transcended boundaries and became an integral part of daily life. Concurrently, other platforms like Twitter, LinkedIn, and YouTube joined the fray, each catering to unique aspects of human expression and connection.

The Evolution of Social Media Platforms

1. Facebook: A Global Social Network

Facebook's journey from a Harvard dorm room project to a global social behemoth reflects the transformative power of social media. The platform not only redefined how we connect with friends and family but also influenced the way businesses engage with their audiences. The introduction of features like the News Feed, Timeline, and the ubiquitous "Like" button transformed Facebook into an ever-evolving ecosystem where personal and professional lives intersect.

2. Twitter: Microblogging and Real-Time Conversations

In 2006, Twitter emerged as a microblogging platform, restricting users to concise 280-character messages. This limitation, rather than hindering communication, fueled the rise of real-time conversations. Twitter became the go-to platform for breaking news, trending topics, and public discourse. Its impact on shaping public opinion and fostering global conversations cannot be overstated.

3. Instagram: Visual Storytelling and Influencer Culture

Instagram, launched in 2010, introduced a novel concept — visual storytelling through images and short videos. Focused on aesthetics and creativity, it quickly became a hub for influencers, shaping trends, and setting societal standards for beauty and lifestyle. Instagram's emphasis on visual content altered the dynamics of self-expression, establishing a new paradigm for digital identity.

4. LinkedIn: Professional Networking in the Digital Age

While platforms like Facebook and Instagram cater to personal connections, LinkedIn carved a niche for itself in the professional realm. Launched in 2003, LinkedIn transformed the job market by providing a digital space for networking, recruitment, and career development. It became an essential tool for professionals seeking new opportunities and businesses scouting for talent.

5. YouTube: The Power of Video Content

YouTube, founded in 2005, disrupted the traditional entertainment industry by democratizing content creation. Anyone with a camera and an internet connection could become a creator, reshaping the dynamics of fame and entertainment. The platform's impact on visual storytelling and its role as an educational resource underscore its influence on shaping perspectives and disseminating information.

The Impact of Social Media on Lives and Relationships

1. Virtual Connectivity and Social Bonds

Social media has revolutionized the concept of connectivity, eradicating geographical barriers and enabling instantaneous communication. Long-distance relationships thrive on platforms like Skype, WhatsApp, and FaceTime, allowing individuals to maintain emotional connections irrespective of physical distances. However, the virtual realm also introduces challenges, as the curated nature of online interactions may lead to misconceptions and misunderstandings.

2. Identity Construction and Self-Image

The digital age has given rise to a culture of personal branding, where individuals meticulously curate their online personas. Social media serves as a canvas for self-expression, but it also raises questions about authenticity. The pressure to conform to societal standards of beauty, success, and happiness can contribute to the phenomenon of "social media anxiety", where individuals feel inadequate compared to the curated lives of others.

3. Impact on Mental Health

The incessant flow of information, the pursuit of validation through likes and comments, and the constant exposure to curated lifestyles contribute to the complex relationship between social media and mental health. Studies indicate correlations between heavy social media use and increased levels of stress, anxiety, and depression. The comparison culture perpetuated by these platforms can exacerbate feelings of inadequacy and isolation.

4. Influence of Social Media on Relationships

Social media's influence extends beyond individual well-being to impact the dynamics of relationships. The public nature of online interactions introduces new challenges, such as navigating digital boundaries, managing online jealousy, and addressing the consequences of online conflicts. On the flip side, social media facilitates new avenues for relationship building, enabling couples to share experiences, create memories, and engage in shared interests.

Conclusion

As we navigate the intricate landscape of social media, it becomes evident that its impact on our lives and relationships is profound and multifaceted. From its humble beginnings as a virtual extension of real-world connections to a global network shaping opinions, trends, and identities, social media has evolved into an integral aspect of contemporary existence.

While the benefits of virtual connectivity and the democratization of information are undeniable, it is crucial to recognize and address the challenges posed by the dark side of social media — the impact on mental health, the pressure to conform to unrealistic standards, and the complexities it introduces into our relationships. Understanding the evolution and implications of social media is paramount as we strive to navigate this digital landscape and harness its potential for positive transformation in our lives and relationships.

Introduction

In the rapidly evolving landscape of the digital age, social media has emerged as a powerful force that influences almost every aspect of our lives. From personal relationships to global events, the impact of platforms like Facebook, Twitter, Instagram, and others is undeniable. This article delves into the journey of social media, exploring its popularity, growth, and the profound ways it shapes our lives and relationships.

Exploring the Popularity and Growth of Social Media

The inception of social media can be traced back to the early 2000s when platforms like Friendster and MySpace paved the way for a new form of online interaction. However, it was the advent of Facebook in 2004 that marked a turning point in the digital landscape. Facebook quickly became a global phenomenon, connecting individuals across continents and revolutionizing the way people communicate.

The popularity of social media lies in its ability to transcend geographical boundaries, enabling individuals to share their lives, thoughts, and experiences with a global audience. Platforms like Twitter introduced the concept of microblogging, allowing users to express themselves in concise messages, fostering real-time conversations and debates. Instagram, with its focus on visual content, created a space for sharing moments through images and short videos.

The growth of social media has been exponential. According to recent statistics, there are over 4.95 billion social media users worldwide, representing nearly 61.4% of the global population. The sheer number of users highlights the ubiquity of social platforms in our daily lives. What began as a means of connecting with friends and family has evolved into a multifaceted tool that influences politics, culture, and even our mental well-being.

Statistics and Demographics of Social Media Users

To truly understand the impact of social media, it's crucial to examine the demographics of its users. While initially perceived as a platform primarily for the younger generation, the user base has become remarkably diverse. Millennials (born between 1981 and 1996) and Generation Z (born between 1996 and 2010) continue to dominate social media, but there is a notable increase in older demographics, with many baby boomers (born between 1946 and 1964) joining platforms to stay connected with their communities.

One of the defining features of social media is its role in shaping public discourse. Political leaders, celebrities, and everyday individuals leverage these platforms to voice their opinions, share information, and engage with a wide audience. Twitter, in particular, has become a political battleground, where policies are discussed, and public sentiment is measured in real-time.

The impact of social media on relationships is multifaceted. On one hand, it has provided a means for long-distance communication, allowing friends and family to stay connected across the globe. Video calls, instant messaging, and the sharing of personal updates create a sense of closeness even when physically apart.

However, the flip side is the potential strain on face-to-face interactions. The prevalence of smartphones and the constant connectivity facilitated by social media have raised concerns about the quality of in-person conversations. The temptation to check notifications or share updates during social gatherings can detract from the present moment, impacting the depth of real-world relationships.

Social media has also transformed the dating landscape. Apps like Tinder and Bumble have redefined how people meet and form romantic connections. The ability to connect with potential partners based on shared interests and preferences has streamlined the dating process, but it has also raised questions about the superficial nature of these connections and the impact on traditional dating norms.

The influence of social media on mental health is a topic of growing concern. The constant exposure to curated images and carefully crafted narratives can contribute to feelings of inadequacy and low self-esteem. The pressure to conform to societal ideals, fueled by the pursuit of likes and validation, has led to a rise in mental health issues, particularly among younger users.

Conclusion

The rise of social media has been nothing short of revolutionary, reshaping the way we communicate, connect, and perceive the world around us. Its impact on relationships, both personal and professional, is profound, influencing the way we form connections, seek information, and navigate the complexities of the digital age.

While social media has undoubtedly brought people together and democratized information, it comes with its own set of challenges. The constant connectivity and curated nature of online interactions raise questions about authenticity and the quality of relationships. As we navigate this digital landscape, it is essential to strike a balance, leveraging the benefits of social media while being mindful of its potential pitfalls.

Ultimately, the evolution of social media is a dynamic process, shaped by the collective actions and interactions of its users. As we continue to witness the impact of these platforms on our lives, it becomes imperative to foster a conscious and responsible approach to social media usage, ensuring that these tools enhance, rather than detract from, the richness of our human connections.

Introduction

In the rapidly evolving landscape of the digital age, social media has emerged as a powerful force shaping the way we perceive ourselves and others. This article delves into the intricate relationship between social media and identity, exploring the profound impact these platforms have on our self-concept and interpersonal relationships. From self-presentation to personal branding, social media plays a multifaceted role in molding our identity in the digital realm.

How Social Media Shapes and Influences Our Self-Identity

Social media platforms serve as digital mirrors reflecting and shaping our self-identity. The constant stream of curated content, status updates, and images contributes to the construction of an online persona, often distinct from our offline selves. The pursuit of likes, comments, and shares becomes a metric for validation, influencing our perception of self-worth.

The concept of the "digital self" takes shape, a carefully crafted version of ourselves tailored to the expectations and norms prevalent on each platform.

The curated nature of social media content introduces a paradoxical dynamic to self-identity. On one hand, individuals may present an idealized version of their lives, showcasing achievements, milestones, and positive experiences. On the other hand, the prevalence of online sharing enables vulnerability and authenticity, with users sharing personal struggles, challenges, and moments of vulnerability. This duality in self-presentation raises questions about the authenticity of the digital self and its impact on our offline identity.

Moreover, the social comparison theory, as articulated by social psychologist Leon Festinger, comes into play on social media. Users are constantly exposed to the lives of others, leading to comparisons that can either bolster or diminish one's self-esteem. The carefully curated nature of content often leads to upward social comparisons, where individuals compare themselves to those seemingly leading more glamorous or successful lives. This phenomenon contributes to the cultivation of unrealistic standards and fosters a culture of comparison that influences how we perceive our own achievements and shortcomings.

The Role of Social Media in Personal Branding

In the age of personal branding, social media serves as a powerful tool for individuals to shape and manage their public image. Platforms like LinkedIn, Instagram, and Twitter allow users to strategically present themselves to a global audience. Personal branding on social media involves a deliberate effort to showcase one's skills, achievements, and values, often with the aim of advancing personal or professional goals.

LinkedIn, for instance, has become a virtual resume and networking hub, where professionals meticulously curate their profiles to attract potential employers or collaborators. The emphasis on highlighting accomplishments and professional expertise transforms the platform into a dynamic space for personal branding. Similarly, Instagram and YouTube provide a visual platform for individuals to establish a brand around their lifestyle, hobbies, or expertise.

However, the pursuit of personal branding on social media raises ethical considerations. The pressure to maintain a curated image can lead to inauthentic self-presentation, blurring the lines between genuine self-expression and performative behavior. The quest for likes and followers can overshadow the authenticity of personal experiences, prompting individuals to prioritize online validation over a true representation of their identity.

Furthermore, personal branding on social media has implications for privacy. The line between public and private becomes increasingly blurred as individuals share intimate aspects of their lives for the sake of personal branding. Striking a balance between authenticity and privacy becomes a complex challenge, as individuals navigate the fine line between sharing meaningful content and preserving the sanctity of personal space.

Conclusion

Social media, with its pervasive influence, significantly shapes and molds our identity in the digital age. The construction of a digital self, influenced by curated content and social comparison, has profound implications for how we perceive ourselves and others. The paradox of authenticity and self-presentation raises questions about the true nature of our online identity and its alignment with our offline selves.

Moreover, the role of social media in personal branding adds another layer to this complex relationship. While it provides a platform for individuals to strategically showcase their skills and achievements, the pursuit of personal branding introduces ethical considerations and challenges related to authenticity and privacy.

As we navigate the ever-evolving landscape of social media, it becomes imperative to critically examine its impact on our identity and relationships. Awareness of the potential pitfalls and opportunities presented by these platforms empowers individuals to engage with social media in a manner that aligns with their values and promotes genuine self-expression. In the digital era, our identity is not only shaped by our offline experiences but is also intricately woven into the fabric of our online presence, making it essential to navigate the virtual realm with mindfulness and authenticity.

Chapter 4. Social Media and Relationships

Introduction

In the contemporary digital age, social media has become an integral part of our daily lives, significantly shaping how we communicate, connect, and relate to others. As we navigate this virtual landscape, it is essential to examine the profound impact social media has on our relationships, encompassing friendships, family bonds, and romantic connections. This exploration unveils the multifaceted ways in which social media influences the dynamics of human relationships.

The Impact of Social Media on Friendships

Social media platforms have revolutionized the way we maintain and cultivate friendships. While these platforms offer unprecedented opportunities to stay connected with friends, they also introduce unique challenges. The concept of a 'friend' has evolved from face-to-face interactions to digital connections, raising questions about the depth and authenticity of these relationships.

One notable effect is the digitization of social circles, with online platforms allowing us to expand our networks globally. However, the sheer volume of connections may dilute the quality of friendships, as digital interactions often lack the depth and intimacy of face-to-face communication. The ease of online communication can foster a sense of disconnection, with individuals opting for convenient digital exchanges over meaningful in-person conversations.

Additionally, the constant stream of curated content on social media can contribute to the phenomenon of social comparison, impacting self-esteem and relationships. Friends may experience envy or feelings of inadequacy when exposed to carefully crafted depictions of others' lives, leading to strained friendships or even the erosion of trust.

How Social Media Affects Family Relationships

Social media's influence extends beyond friendships to reshape family dynamics.

Platforms like Facebook, Instagram, and WhatsApp facilitate communication and sharing among family members, transcending geographical barriers. Yet, this digital connectivity introduces its own set of challenges.

Family relationships are not immune to the pitfalls of social comparison. Parents may feel pressure to measure up to idealized portrayals of other families, while children may develop unrealistic expectations based on curated content. This dynamic can strain familial bonds, as the gap between reality and digital representation widens.

Moreover, the constant connectivity enabled by social media may blur the boundaries between personal and familial space. Privacy becomes a delicate balance as family members navigate the fine line between sharing and oversharing, raising concerns about the erosion of personal boundaries within the family unit.

How Social Media Affects Romantic Relationships and Dating

The impact of social media on romantic relationships is perhaps most palpable, with platforms influencing how we initiate, nurture, and sometimes end intimate connections. The digital realm introduces both opportunities and challenges, transforming the landscape of modern dating.

One significant aspect is the advent of online dating platforms, which have reshaped the way people meet and form romantic connections. While these platforms offer access to a broader pool of potential partners, they also raise questions about the authenticity of online personas and the potential for deception.

Social media's role in relationships extends beyond initial courtship, affecting how couples maintain their connections. The constant connectivity can foster increased communication but may also lead to issues such as jealousy, mistrust, and miscommunication. The public nature of social media introduces a performative aspect to relationships, as couples navigate the balance between sharing their love and maintaining a sense of privacy.

Moreover, social media can become a double-edged sword during relationship challenges. Public disputes, breakup announcements, and emotional posts can contribute to the deterioration of relationships and expose intimate aspects of one's personal life to a wider audience.

Conclusion

As we navigate the intricate web of social media and relationships, it is evident that the digital landscape has both enhanced and complicated our connections with others. Friendships are no longer confined to physical proximity, but the challenge lies in maintaining their depth and authenticity. Family bonds benefit from digital connectivity, yet the blurring of boundaries poses risks to privacy and individual autonomy. Romantic relationships, influenced by the performative nature of social media, require careful navigation to balance connection with discretion.

Ultimately, understanding the impact of social media on relationships is crucial for developing strategies to mitigate its negative effects while harnessing its potential for fostering meaningful connections. As we continue to integrate social media into our lives, the key lies in finding a harmonious balance between the virtual and the real, ensuring that our digital interactions enhance rather than detract from the richness of our relationships.

Introduction

In the contemporary digital landscape, social media has become an inseparable part of our lives, profoundly influencing how we connect, communicate, and perceive the world. As we immerse ourselves in the virtual realm, it's crucial to explore the intricate relationship between social media use and mental health. This article delves into the impact of social media on our well-being, examining the potential challenges it poses and offering strategies for maintaining mental health in the age of constant connectivity.

The Relationship Between Social Media Use and Mental Health Issues

1. Social Comparison and Self-Esteem

Social media platforms often serve as a stage for individuals to showcase curated versions of their lives. This tendency can foster social comparison, leading to feelings of inadequacy and diminished self-esteem.

Users may find themselves constantly measuring their accomplishments against the highlight reels of others, perpetuating a cycle of dissatisfaction.

2. Fear of Missing Out (FOMO)

The constant stream of updates on social media can contribute to the pervasive Fear of Missing Out (FOMO). Seeing friends and peers engaging in exciting activities can lead to feelings of exclusion and loneliness, intensifying the impact on mental health. Understanding the curated nature of social media content is crucial in mitigating the detrimental effects of FOMO.

3. Cyberbullying and Online Harassment

The anonymity afforded by social media can sometimes lead to negative behaviors such as cyberbullying and online harassment. Victimization in the virtual realm can have severe consequences on mental health, causing stress, anxiety, and even depression. Addressing this issue involves fostering a culture of respect and empathy online.

Excessive use of social media can escalate into addiction, impacting mental health by reducing productivity, disrupting sleep patterns, and contributing to a sense of isolation. Establishing healthy boundaries and being mindful of screen time are essential in preventing social media from becoming a compulsive and detrimental habit.

Strategies for Maintaining Mental Well-being in the Social Media Age

1. Mindful Consumption

Being mindful of the content we consume on social media is crucial for mental well-being. Actively curate your feed to include content that inspires, educates, and uplifts. Unfollow accounts that trigger negative emotions and consciously choose to engage with content that promotes positivity.

2. Digital Detox

Recognizing the need for a break from social media is a vital aspect of maintaining mental health. Schedule regular digital detox periods where you disconnect from social platforms, allowing yourself to rejuvenate and focus on in-person connections and activities.

3. Establishing Boundaries

Setting boundaries around social media use is essential for preventing it from encroaching on other aspects of life. Establish specific times for checking social media, and avoid using it during designated periods such as meals, family time, and before bedtime.

4. Cultivating Real-world Connections

While social media facilitates online connections, nurturing real-world relationships is equally important. Invest time in face-to-face interactions, fostering genuine connections that contribute positively to mental well-being. Balancing online and offline relationships helps create a more holistic social experience.

5. Promoting Digital Literacy

Educating individuals about digital literacy can empower them to navigate social media more responsibly. Understanding the curated nature of online content, recognizing misinformation, and being aware of the potential impact of social comparison can contribute to a healthier online experience.

Conclusion

In the evolving landscape of social media, its impact on mental health cannot be underestimated. The constant influx of information and the curated nature of online interactions can contribute to a range of mental health issues. However, by adopting mindful practices, establishing boundaries, and promoting digital literacy, individuals can navigate the digital realm more effectively.

Acknowledging the potential challenges and proactively addressing them is essential for harnessing the positive aspects of social media while safeguarding our mental well-being. Striking a balance between the virtual and real-world connections, practicing digital detox, and fostering a culture of empathy online are pivotal steps toward ensuring that social media enhances rather than detracts from our lives.

As we continue to grapple with the ever-evolving landscape of social media, it is imperative to approach it with a critical and conscious mindset. By understanding the nuances of the relationship between social media and mental health, we can cultivate a digital environment that promotes positive connections, personal growth, and overall well-being.

Chapter 6. Cyberbullying and Online Harassment

Introduction

Social media has undeniably transformed the way we connect, communicate, and build relationships. It has opened up new avenues for self-expression, networking, and information sharing. However, as our lives become increasingly entwined with these digital platforms, a darker side has emerged – the realm of cyberbullying and online harassment. This article delves into the nuances of this pervasive issue, exploring its roots, impact, and potential solutions.

Understanding the Dark Side of Social Media

1. The Evolution of Cyberbullying

Cyberbullying has evolved with the rapid growth of social media. What once may have been confined to schoolyards now extends into the virtual space, where individuals can be targeted relentlessly. The cloak of anonymity emboldens perpetrators, amplifying the impact of their actions. From hurtful comments and derogatory messages to the malicious spread of misinformation, the tactics employed in cyberbullying are as varied as they are damaging.

2. Impact on Mental Health

The consequences of cyberbullying are far-reaching, particularly on mental health. Victims often experience anxiety, depression, and even contemplate self-harm. The constant barrage of negative messages, coupled with the feeling of being relentlessly pursued online, can lead to a profound sense of isolation and despair. Social media, once a tool for connection, becomes a breeding ground for emotional distress.

3. The Role of Social Media Platforms

While social media platforms have provided a stage for cyberbullying, they also play a pivotal role in shaping its contours. Algorithms designed to maximize engagement can inadvertently fuel the spread of harmful content. The ease with which information can be shared and manipulated on these platforms contributes to the rapid escalation of online harassment. Recognizing this, many platforms have implemented measures to curb abuse, but the effectiveness of these efforts remains a subject of ongoing debate.

Coping with and Combating Online Harassment

1. Empowering the Victims

One of the first steps in combating online harassment is empowering the victims. Encouraging individuals to speak out against cyberbullying helps break the silence surrounding the issue. Sharing personal experiences not only provides a support network for victims but also raises awareness about the pervasive nature of online harassment.

2. Education and Digital Literacy

Education plays a crucial role in mitigating the impact of cyberbullying. Incorporating digital literacy programs into school curricula can equip students with the tools to navigate the online world responsibly. Teaching them to discern between constructive criticism and harmful behavior can foster a healthier online environment.

Implementing robust online safety measures is essential in preventing and addressing cyberbullying. Social media platforms must actively enforce policies against harassment, hate speech, and other forms of abusive behavior. Regular audits and updates to these policies ensure that they remain relevant in an ever-evolving digital landscape.

4. Promoting Positive Online Behavior

Creating a positive online culture requires the collective efforts of users, communities, and platform developers. Encouraging respectful and inclusive behavior can counteract the toxicity that often permeates social media. The promotion of empathy and understanding is crucial in fostering a virtual space where individuals feel safe expressing themselves without fear of reprisal.

Conclusion

As social media continues to shape our lives and relationships, addressing the issue of cyberbullying and online harassment becomes increasingly urgent. The consequences of inaction are profound, affecting not only the mental health of individuals but also the fabric of our digital society. Recognizing the dark side of social media is the first step towards mitigating its impact.

Combatting cyberbullying requires a multi-faceted approach, involving individuals, communities, and the platforms themselves. Empowering victims, promoting digital literacy, implementing online safety measures, and fostering positive online behavior are all integral components of a comprehensive strategy.

In the ongoing narrative of social media's influence on our lives, it is imperative that we steer it towards a future where these platforms serve as conduits for positive engagement and connection. Only through collective awareness, education, and concerted efforts can we hope to create a digital landscape where individuals thrive without the shadows of cyberbullying looming over them.

Introduction

In the contemporary digital age, social media has become an integral part of our daily lives, influencing how we connect, communicate, and consume information. One of the most significant realms where the impact of social media is palpable is in the arena of politics. This article explores the multifaceted role of social media in shaping political opinions, the challenges posed by the spread of misinformation, and ultimately, how these dynamics influence our lives and relationships.

The Role of Social Media in Shaping Political Opinions

Social media platforms serve as dynamic spaces where political conversations unfold in real-time. These platforms offer users a voice, enabling them to express their opinions, engage with political content, and connect with like-minded individuals. Twitter, Facebook, Instagram, and other platforms have become powerful tools for political activism, providing a space for grassroots movements to mobilize and gain momentum.

Politicians and political parties leverage social media to connect directly with constituents, bypassing traditional media channels. This direct communication fosters a sense of accessibility, making political figures seem more relatable and accountable. However, this also opens the door to a more personalized and often polarized political discourse.

The echo chamber effect is a notable consequence of social media's role in shaping political opinions. Algorithms curate content based on users' preferences, creating echo chambers where individuals are exposed to information that aligns with their existing beliefs. This can reinforce existing biases, limit exposure to diverse perspectives, and contribute to the polarization of political discourse.

Moreover, the virality of content on social media amplifies the impact of political messages. A single tweet or post can reach millions of users within seconds, influencing public opinion on a massive scale. The immediacy of these platforms accelerates the pace at which political narratives evolve and shape public discourse.

The Spread of Misinformation and Its Consequences

While social media has democratized information dissemination, it has also become a breeding ground for misinformation and fake news. The rapid spread of false or misleading information poses a significant challenge to the integrity of political discourse and decision-making.

The ease with which misinformation spreads on social media can be attributed to various factors. The absence of gatekeepers, the viral nature of content, and algorithmic biases contribute to the unchecked proliferation of false information. This, in turn, has profound implications for public perception, as individuals may form opinions based on inaccurate or incomplete information.

Foreign interference in elections is another consequence of the interconnected nature of social media. State actors and external entities exploit these platforms to disseminate propaganda, manipulate public opinion, and undermine the democratic process. The anonymity afforded by social media makes it challenging to trace the origins of such interference, adding a layer of complexity to addressing this issue.

The consequences of misinformation extend beyond the digital realm. In extreme cases, false information propagated on social media can incite real-world violence or contribute to the erosion of trust in institutions. The impact of misinformation on political stability and the health of democratic societies underscores the need for vigilant efforts to combat its spread.

Addressing the challenge of misinformation requires a multi-faceted approach. Social media platforms must invest in robust fact-checking mechanisms, algorithmic transparency, and user education to empower individuals to discern reliable information from falsehoods. Collaborative efforts between platforms, governments, and civil society are essential to mitigate the adverse effects of misinformation on the political landscape.

Conclusion

Social media's influence on politics is undeniable, shaping the way we form opinions, engage with information, and participate in democratic processes. While these platforms offer unprecedented opportunities for political expression and mobilization, they also present challenges such as echo chambers and the spread of misinformation.

As we navigate the complex intersection of social media and politics, it is crucial to strike a balance between fostering open dialogue and mitigating the negative consequences. Social media platforms, policymakers, and users alike must collaborate to create an environment where diverse perspectives are valued, misinformation is curtailed, and the democratic ideals that underpin our societies are preserved.

In the ever-evolving landscape of social media and politics, the choices we make today will shape the future of our lives and relationships. By understanding the dynamics at play and actively working towards responsible engagement, we can harness the positive potential of social media while mitigating its pitfalls in the realm of politics.

Introduction

In the modern age, social media has become an integral part of our lives, shaping how we communicate, share information, and build relationships. However, the pervasive influence of social media raises significant concerns about privacy. The digital era has brought about a new paradigm where personal information is often willingly shared, sometimes without a full understanding of the potential consequences. This article explores the intricate relationship between social media and privacy, delving into the concerns surrounding data privacy and providing insights into how individuals can safeguard their online presence.

Concerns about Data Privacy and Social Media

1. The Digital Footprint Dilemma

One of the foremost concerns associated with social media is the creation of a digital footprint. Every click, like, comment, and share contributes to a user's digital footprint, a trail of data that can be harnessed by social media platforms for various purposes. While these platforms use this data to tailor user experiences and deliver targeted content, it also raises questions about the extent to which individuals are willing to trade privacy for convenience.

2. Data Monetization and Advertising

Social media platforms thrive on user engagement, and this engagement is monetized through targeted advertising. Algorithms analyze user behavior and preferences, allowing advertisers to tailor their messages with remarkable precision. However, the flip side of this customization is the potential invasion of privacy. Users may feel as though their every move is being watched, raising concerns about the ethical use of personal data for financial gain.

3. Third-Party Data Sharing

Beyond the realms of social media platforms, the data collected is often shared with third-party entities. This includes advertisers, analytics firms, and other organizations eager to tap into the vast reservoirs of user information. This practice not only poses privacy risks but also highlights the complex web of data sharing that occurs in the digital ecosystem, sometimes without users' explicit consent.

4. Security Breaches and Hacking

In the era of constant connectivity, security breaches and hacking incidents have become a stark reality. Social media platforms, holding troves of personal information, are prime targets for cybercriminals. High-profile breaches have exposed the vulnerability of these platforms, prompting individuals to question the safety of their personal data and whether the convenience of social media is worth the potential risks.

How to Protect Your Privacy Online

1. Review and Adjust Privacy Settings

The first line of defense against privacy concerns on social media is to understand and utilize the platform's privacy settings. Most platforms offer a range of customizable options that allow users to control who sees their information. Regularly reviewing and adjusting these settings can help individuals fine-tune their online presence, striking a balance between sharing and protecting personal information.

2. Be Mindful of Sharing Personal Information

While it may seem obvious, being mindful of the information shared online is crucial. Oversharing details such as addresses, phone numbers, or financial information can expose individuals to various risks, including identity theft and cyberstalking. A conscious effort to limit the disclosure of sensitive information can go a long way in protecting one's privacy.

3. Use Two-Factor Authentication

Enhancing the security of social media accounts is essential in safeguarding personal information. Two-factor authentication adds an extra layer of protection by requiring a secondary verification step, typically through a text message or authentication app. This additional hurdle makes it more difficult for unauthorized individuals to gain access to an account, reducing the risk of privacy breaches.

4. Regularly Update Passwords

Password hygiene is a fundamental aspect of online security. Regularly updating passwords and using strong, unique combinations can help prevent unauthorized access to social media accounts. Reusing passwords across multiple platforms is a common pitfall that can amplify the impact of a security breach. Adopting a password manager can streamline the process of maintaining strong, varied passwords for different accounts.

5. Educate Yourself on Platform Policies

Understanding the privacy policies and terms of service of social media platforms is crucial. These documents outline how user data is collected, used, and shared. Being informed about these policies empowers users to make conscious decisions about their online presence. In some cases, users may choose to opt out of certain data collection practices or limit the visibility of their information.

6. Limit Third-Party App Permissions

Many social media platforms allow third-party apps to access user data. While these apps may enhance functionality, they can also pose privacy risks. Reviewing and limiting the permissions granted to third-party apps can help mitigate these risks. Removing apps that are no longer needed can also reduce the potential exposure of personal information.

Conclusion

In the ever-evolving landscape of social media, the intertwining of technology and personal life raises profound questions about privacy. While the concerns are valid, it's crucial to acknowledge that social media is not inherently malicious. Rather, it is a tool that, when used mindfully, can enrich our lives and relationships.

Balancing the benefits and risks of social media requires individual responsibility and collective awareness. As users, we must be vigilant about the information we share, educate ourselves about platform policies, and employ security measures to protect our digital selves. Simultaneously, the evolving landscape of digital ethics calls for continued scrutiny of platform practices, advocating for transparent policies and ethical use of user data.

Ultimately, the journey of social media and privacy is a dynamic one. As technology advances and societal norms evolve, the dialogue around privacy will continue to shape the digital landscape. By fostering a culture of informed consent, responsible use, and technological literacy, individuals can navigate the complexities of social media while safeguarding their privacy in the digital age.

Chapter 9. Addiction and Dependency

Introduction

In the age of digitization, social media has become an integral part of our daily lives, shaping the way we communicate, connect, and consume information. While these platforms offer unprecedented opportunities for networking and self-expression, a darker side looms – the potential for addiction and dependency. This article delves into the intricate web of social media's addictive nature, explores the psychological underpinnings, and provides practical tips for managing social media usage to foster healthier relationships.

The Addictive Nature of Social Media

1. Dopamine Rush and Reward System

Social media platforms are expertly designed to trigger the release of dopamine, a neurotransmitter associated with pleasure and reward. Likes, comments, and shares act as virtual affirmations, creating a sense of accomplishment and satisfaction. This constant positive reinforcement contributes to the addictive cycle, compelling users to seek more engagement and validation.

2. Fear of Missing Out (FOMO)

The curated nature of social media feeds often leads to the "Fear of Missing Out" phenomenon. Users scroll through carefully curated content, witnessing the highlight reels of others' lives, fostering a sense of inadequacy and the need to stay connected at all times. This fear becomes a powerful driver, keeping individuals glued to their screens in a perpetual quest for updates and connection.

3. Infinite Scroll and Endless Engagement

The infinite scroll feature, present in most social media interfaces, encourages continuous scrolling, creating an endless loop of content consumption. This design choice taps into the psychological concept of variable rewards, where users never know what they might encounter next. This unpredictability sustains engagement, making it challenging for individuals to disengage from the platform voluntarily.

Tips for Managing Social Media Usage

1. Set Boundaries and Time Limits

Establishing clear boundaries is crucial in managing social media usage. Define specific time slots for engagement and stick to them. Use features like app timers or third-party apps to set daily limits, ensuring that social media doesn't encroach on other essential aspects of your life.

2. Curate Your Feed Mindfully

Take control of your social media experience by curating your feed intentionally. Unfollow accounts that contribute to negative feelings or induce comparison. Follow content creators and communities that inspire, educate, and align with your interests, creating a more positive and uplifting digital environment.

3. Practice Mindful Consumption

Be conscious of your social media consumption patterns. Instead of mindlessly scrolling, engage with content mindfully. Reflect on how each post makes you feel and whether it adds value to your life. This mindful approach fosters a healthier relationship with social media, reducing the risk of addiction.

4. Designate Tech-Free Zones

Create designated tech-free zones in your daily routine, such as during meals or before bedtime. This intentional break allows you to disconnect from the virtual world and reconnect with the present moment, promoting a more balanced and fulfilling lifestyle.

Conclusion

Social media's impact on our lives and relationships is profound, with addiction and dependency emerging as significant challenges. Understanding the psychological mechanisms at play is the first step toward cultivating a healthier relationship with these platforms. By implementing practical strategies such as setting boundaries, curating content mindfully, and practicing mindful consumption, individuals can regain control over their social media usage and foster more meaningful connections in the digital age. Ultimately, striking a balance between the virtual and real worlds is key to harnessing the benefits of social media while mitigating its potential negative effects on our well-being and relationships.

Introduction

Parenting in the Social Media Age presents a unique set of challenges and opportunities, reshaping the landscape of how families interact, communicate, and form relationships. As technology becomes increasingly integrated into our daily lives, the impact on parenting styles and the dynamics within families cannot be overlooked. This article explores the multifaceted aspects of parenting in the digital era, focusing on the challenges of raising children in a world dominated by social media and the importance of striking a balance between screen time and real-world experiences.

Navigating the Challenges of Raising Children in a Digital World

In this digital age, children are growing up with unprecedented access to information and connectivity. While this opens up a world of possibilities, it also poses challenges for parents trying to navigate the fine line between granting autonomy and ensuring responsible online behavior. One of the primary concerns is the potential exposure to inappropriate content, cyberbullying, and the pressure to conform to unrealistic standards propagated by social media.

Parents find themselves grappling with questions like, "How much screen time is too much?" and "How can I protect my child from the negative aspects of online interactions?" Establishing open lines of communication with children becomes crucial in addressing these concerns. Regular conversations about online safety, the responsible use of social media, and the potential consequences of inappropriate behavior can empower children to make informed decisions in the digital realm.

Additionally, parents must stay informed about the latest trends and platforms their children are using. Keeping up with the ever-evolving landscape of social media allows parents to better understand the challenges their children may face and guide them through potential pitfalls.

Balancing Screen Time and Real-World Experiences

While the digital age has brought about remarkable advancements, it is essential to strike a balance between screen time and real-world experiences. Excessive screen time can impact children's physical health, mental well-being, and social development. As parents, fostering a healthy relationship with technology involves setting clear boundaries, encouraging outdoor activities, and promoting face-to-face interactions.

Establishing designated screen-free times, such as during family meals or before bedtime, creates opportunities for meaningful connections within the family. This not only reduces the potential negative effects of excessive screen time but also reinforces the importance of in-person relationships.

Encouraging real-world experiences also involves supporting children in developing hobbies and interests outside the digital realm. Whether it's sports, arts, or community involvement, these activities contribute to a well-rounded upbringing and help children cultivate skills beyond the virtual world. Parents can play an active role in identifying and nurturing their children's passions, fostering a sense of purpose that extends beyond the confines of social media.

Furthermore, leading by example is paramount. Parents must model healthy technology use, demonstrating the importance of unplugging and engaging in offline activities. This not only reinforces the value of a balanced lifestyle but also provides children with a positive template for their own behavior.

Conclusion

Parenting in the Social Media Age is a delicate balancing act, requiring adaptability, communication, and a proactive approach to the challenges posed by the digital world. While social media offers unprecedented opportunities for connection and self-expression, it also introduces new complexities and potential risks. Navigating these challenges involves staying informed, fostering open communication, and actively participating in the online and offline aspects of children's lives.

The key to successful parenting in the digital era lies in finding the right balance between screen time and real-world experiences. By setting boundaries, encouraging offline activities, and modeling responsible technology use, parents can guide their children toward a healthy relationship with the digital realm. As technology continues to shape our lives and relationships, it is essential for parents to remain vigilant, adaptable, and engaged in their children's digital journeys, ensuring a harmonious integration of the virtual and real worlds.

Chapter 11. The Business of Social Media

Introduction

In the digital age, social media has become an integral part of our daily lives, profoundly influencing how we connect, communicate, and consume information. Beyond its role in shaping personal relationships, social media has emerged as a powerful force in the business realm, transforming the way companies operate, market their products, and engage with consumers. This article delves into the multifaceted world of the business of social media, exploring its economic impact, the dynamics of social media marketing, and the profound influence it exerts on consumer behavior.

The Economic Impact of Social Media

Social media platforms have evolved into bustling digital marketplaces, serving as fertile grounds for economic transactions and business activities. The economic impact of social media is far-reaching, touching various aspects of commerce and trade.

1. Job Creation and Industry Growth

The rise of social media has given birth to entirely new industries, ranging from content creation and influencer marketing to social media management. As businesses strive to establish their digital presence, a demand for skilled professionals in areas like digital marketing, content creation, and social media strategy has surged. This has not only created job opportunities but also fueled economic growth in related sectors.

2. Digital Advertising Revenue

Advertising, a cornerstone of business promotion, has found new avenues through social media platforms. Companies allocate substantial budgets to digital advertising on platforms such as Facebook, Instagram, and Twitter, leveraging the vast user base to reach their target audiences. The revenue generated by social media advertising has become a significant contributor to the overall digital advertising landscape.

3. E-commerce Integration

Social media has seamlessly integrated with e-commerce, blurring the lines between online engagement and shopping. Platforms like Instagram and Pinterest allow businesses to showcase products directly, providing a convenient shopping experience for users. The 'shop now' features and integrated payment gateways have turned social media into a thriving marketplace.

Social Media Marketing and Its Influence on Consumer Behavior

The advent of social media has revolutionized marketing strategies, necessitating a shift from traditional approaches to dynamic and interactive methods. Social media marketing has emerged as a potent tool, not only for brand promotion but also for shaping consumer behavior.

1. Building Brand Identity and Awareness

Social media serves as a virtual storefront, allowing businesses to craft and project their brand identity. Through engaging content, storytelling, and consistent interaction with followers, companies can establish a strong online presence. This, in turn, fosters brand awareness and loyalty, vital components of successful marketing strategies.

2. Influencer Marketing

The era of influencers has ushered in a new dimension to social media marketing. Individuals with significant followings, known as influencers, collaborate with brands to promote products or services. The personal and authentic touch that influencers bring to their endorsements resonates with audiences, influencing purchasing decisions and shaping consumer trends.

3. Targeted Advertising and Analytics

Social media platforms leverage user data to facilitate targeted advertising, allowing businesses to tailor their messages to specific demographics. The use of analytics tools provides valuable insights into consumer behavior, preferences, and engagement patterns. This data-driven approach enables businesses to refine their marketing strategies for maximum impact.

Social media's real-time nature facilitates direct communication between brands and consumers. Companies can engage with their audience through comments, direct messages, and interactive content. This immediate feedback loop not only strengthens customer relationships but also provides valuable insights into consumer sentiment, aiding businesses in adapting and evolving their offerings.

Conclusion

The business of social media is a dynamic and ever-evolving landscape that continues to shape our economic and social interactions. From job creation and industry growth to the transformation of marketing strategies, social media's influence is pervasive. As we navigate this interconnected digital realm, it becomes imperative for businesses to harness the power of social media strategically.

The economic impact of social media is not just about revenue figures; it extends to the fabric of our society, influencing how we perceive brands, make purchasing decisions, and connect with each other. As we move forward, businesses must adapt to the changing landscape, leveraging the opportunities presented by social media to foster innovation, customer engagement, and sustainable growth. In this intricate dance between technology and society, the business of social media plays a central role in shaping the way we live, work, and relate to one another.

Chapter 12. The Future of Social Media

Introduction

In the ever-evolving landscape of technology, social media stands as a powerful force shaping the way we communicate, connect, and relate to the world around us. As we navigate through the current digital era, it is crucial to explore the emerging trends and technologies that are molding the future of social media and, consequently, influencing the fabric of our lives and relationships.

The Current State of Social Media

Before delving into the future, it's essential to understand the present state of social media. Platforms like Facebook, Instagram, Twitter, and LinkedIn have become integral parts of our daily routines, allowing us to share experiences, connect with friends and family, and engage with a global community. However, the landscape is not static. The dynamism of technology ensures that social media is in a perpetual state of evolution.

Emerging Trends in Social Media

1. Augmented Reality (AR) and Virtual Reality (VR)

The integration of AR and VR technologies into social media platforms is transforming the user experience. Imagine attending a virtual concert or exploring a museum exhibit from the comfort of your living room. Social media is poised to become more immersive, blurring the lines between the physical and digital realms.

2. Artificial Intelligence (AI) and Personalization

AI is enhancing the personalization of content on social media. Algorithms analyze user behavior, preferences, and interactions to tailor content, ensuring that individuals receive information and updates relevant to their interests. This move towards hyper-personalization not only keeps users engaged but also raises concerns about privacy and the echo chamber effect.

3. Ephemeral Content

The rise of ephemeral content, epitomized by the Stories feature on platforms like Instagram and Snapchat, reflects a shift towards more casual and spontaneous sharing. This trend challenges the traditional permanence of social media posts, encouraging authenticity and impermanence in our digital interactions.

Speculations on the Future Impact of Social Media

1. Redefining Relationships

The future of social media is likely to redefine the nature of relationships. As virtual interactions become more immersive and lifelike, people may form deep connections with others across geographical boundaries. This could lead to a transformation in how we perceive friendship, love, and community, with digital relationships carrying equal weight to those forged in the physical world.

2. Mental Health and Well-being

While social media has connected us in unprecedented ways, concerns about its impact on mental health persist. The future holds the promise of more empathetic and supportive social media environments. Machine learning algorithms could be designed to detect signs of distress and offer resources or connect users with mental health professionals. Striking a balance between connectivity and well-being will be crucial.

3. Social Activism and Change

Social media has already proven to be a powerful tool for social activism and change. Looking ahead, platforms may play an even more significant role in mobilizing movements, raising awareness, and fostering global solidarity. The ability to amplify diverse voices and highlight social issues could lead to positive societal shifts, facilitated by the connectivity provided by these platforms.

4. Privacy and Ethical Concerns

As social media becomes more intertwined with our daily lives, privacy concerns are likely to intensify. Stricter regulations and increased user awareness may prompt platforms to adopt more transparent practices regarding data collection and usage. Balancing the benefits of personalization with ethical considerations will be a continual challenge.

Conclusion

The future of social media holds both promise and challenges. As we navigate this ever-changing landscape, it is essential to stay vigilant about the impact on our lives and relationships. The evolving technologies, from AR and VR to AI, will undoubtedly reshape the way we connect and communicate. Redefining relationships, addressing mental health concerns, and leveraging social media for positive societal change are pivotal considerations.

The responsibility lies not only with the developers and platform creators but also with the users. Understanding the implications of our digital interactions and advocating for a healthier, more inclusive online environment will be crucial. The future of social media is in our hands, and by steering it in the right direction, we can ensure that these platforms continue to enhance our lives and relationships rather than hinder them.

"How Social Media Shapes Our Lives and Relationships" delves into the profound impact of social media on our modern existence, exploring its evolution, prevalence, and consequences. The journey begins with an 'Introduction to Social Media', providing a historical overview and tracing the development of various platforms. 'The Rise of Social Media' investigates its popularity and growth through compelling statistics and demographics. Chapters such as 'Social Media and Identity' and 'Social Media and Relationships' examine how these platforms influence our self-perception and interpersonal connections.

'Social Media and Mental Health' and 'Cyberbullying and Online Harassment' confront the darker aspects, offering insights into maintaining mental well-being and combating online threats. 'Social Media and Politics' scrutinizes its role in shaping opinions, while 'Social Media and Privacy' addresses concerns about data protection. The book further explores addiction, parenting challenges in the digital age, the business impact, and concludes with a speculative gaze into 'The Future of Social Media', anticipating emerging trends and technologies. Engaging and informative, this book serves as a comprehensive guide to navigating the complex landscape of social media in our interconnected world.

ABOUT THE AUTHOR

Mr. C. P. Kumar is a retired Scientist 'G' from National Institute of Hydrology, Roorkee, Uttarakhand, India. He is also a Reiki Healer and Chakra Balancing practitioner (with pendulum dowsing) and offers Emotional Freedom Technique (EFT) to help individuals with emotional issues. Mr. Kumar has authored many books on technical, spiritual, and social topics.

For further details, you may visit his webpage https://www.angelfire.com/nh/cpkumar/virgo.html

www.ingramcontent.com/pod-product-compliance
Lightning Source LLC
Chambersburg PA
CBHW061351140726

47997CB00003B/1162